CONSULTING PRO:

Navigating The Road To Success

Dack Douglas

Icon Publications Limited

FOREWORD

Welcome to "Consulting Pro: Navigating The Road To Success," where your expertise, passion, and guidance have the power to transform businesses and lives. In this book, we embark on a journey together to explore the art of starting a successful consulting business.

Consulting is not just a profession; it's a calling to make a difference. Whether you're an experienced professional looking to share your knowledge or an aspiring entrepreneur eager to carve your path, this book will serve as your compass, guiding you through the intricacies of building a thriving consulting venture.

Throughout these pages, you will find valuable insights, practical tips, and real-life anecdotes that draw from the collective wisdom of seasoned consultants. From defining your niche and crafting your unique value proposition to mastering the art of client acquisition and delivering exceptional results, we cover it all.

Starting a consulting business can be both rewarding and challenging, and I encourage you to embrace the learning journey ahead. As you delve into the chapters that follow, remember that success in consulting lies not just in your expertise but also in your ability to build meaningful relationships and constantly adapt to the ever-changing business landscape.

As you absorb the knowledge within these pages, let it empower you to unleash your potential as a consultant. May this book be your trusty companion, inspiring you to reach new heights of success, impact, and fulfillment in the consulting world.

Best of luck on your consulting adventure!

Dack Douglas

CONTENTS

CHAPTER 1:
The Evolving Landscape of Consulting

Key Components In Becoming A Great Consultant

1. Specialize: Identify a niche or specific area of expertise that sets you apart from others in the industry. Become an expert in that domain.

2. Continuous Learning: Stay up-to-date with the latest trends, technologies, and methodologies in the consulting field to offer innovative solutions to clients.

3. Networking: Build a strong professional network to connect with potential clients and collaborators. Attend industry events, join online forums, and engage with relevant communities.

4. Personal Branding: Establish a strong online presence through a professional website, blog, or social media platforms. Showcase your expertise and share valuable insights.

5. Client-Centric Approach: Focus on understanding your clients' needs and deliver tailored solutions to meet their specific challenges.

6. Value Proposition: Clearly communicate the unique value you bring to clients and how your services can solve their problems effectively.

7. Flexibility and Adaptability: Be open to adapting your approach based on changing market dynamics and client requirements.

8. Case Studies and Testimonials: Collect and showcase success stories from previous consulting engagements to demonstrate your effectiveness.

9. Collaboration: Partner with other consultants or firms to combine expertise and expand your service offerings.

10. Ethics and Integrity: Maintain high ethical standards, as trust and credibility are crucial in the consulting industry.

Remember, carving your path in consulting takes time, persistence, and a commitment to continuous improvement. Stay focused on delivering value to clients, and your reputation will help pave the way for future success.

Understanding The Benefits And Challenges Of Becoming A Consultant

Becoming a consultant can be a transformative journey, offering both enticing benefits and formidable challenges.

Embarking on the Benefits:

1. Freedom of Choice: As a consultant, you have the freedom to choose your projects, clients, and work schedule, empowering you to strike a work-life balance that suits your preferences.

2. Diverse Opportunities: The consulting realm exposes you to diverse industries, challenges, and cutting-edge solutions, fostering continuous learning and personal growth.

3. Impactful Contributions: Consultants often witness the direct impact of their expertise, making a tangible difference in clients' businesses and witnessing the fruits of their labor.\
4. Networking and Exposure: Engaging with various clients and colleagues nurtures an extensive professional network, opening doors to new prospects and collaborations.

5. Financial Rewards: Successful consultants can enjoy higher earning potential, especially when they establish themselves as experts in sought-after domains.

Navigating the Challenges:

1. Uncertain Income: In the initial stages, irregular cash flow can pose financial challenges, necessitating budgeting and financial planning for stability.

2. Client Acquisition: Attracting and retaining clients demands consistent effort in marketing, networking, and showcasing your expertise.

3. Time Management: Balancing multiple projects and deadlines requires effective time management and the ability to prioritize tasks efficiently.

4. Continuous Adaptation: The consulting landscape evolves rapidly, requiring constant adaptation to stay ahead of emerging trends and technologies.

5. Managing Expectations: Clients may have high expectations, making it crucial to manage and meet their requirements while maintaining realistic goals.

6. Workload Peaks: Intense project demands may lead to periods of high workload, necessitating resilience and stress management.

7. Competitive Environment: The consulting arena can be highly competitive, requiring you to differentiate yourself and stand out in a crowded marketplace.

To thrive as a consultant, embrace the challenges as opportunities for growth, leverage your strengths, and remain steadfast in your commitment to delivering exceptional value to clients. Success comes not just from overcoming obstacles but from your ability to envision a unique path and navigate it with passion and purpose.

Defining Your Consulting Niche And Value Proposition

Discovering your consulting niche and crafting a compelling value proposition is akin to sculpting your business identity - a process that demands creativity, introspection, and market awareness.

Carving Your Consulting Niche:

1. Self-Reflection: Begin by exploring your passions, skills, and expertise. Assess your unique strengths and experiences to identify the areas where you can offer the most value.

2. Market Research: Investigate industry trends, client needs, and potential gaps in the market. Look for areas where your expertise aligns with unmet demands.

3. Uniqueness and Differentiation: Seek a niche that allows you to stand out from competitors. Embrace your individuality and explore how your

approach can solve problems distinctively.

4. Test and Iterate: Don't be afraid to experiment with different niches. Test the waters with pilot projects to gain insights into what resonates most with your target audience.

Crafting Your Value Proposition:

1. Client-Centric Approach: Focus on the outcomes and benefits you provide to clients rather than just your services. Address their pain points and demonstrate how you can alleviate them.

2. Unique Solution: Clearly communicate what sets your consulting apart from others. Highlight your distinctive methodology or approach that leads to better results.

3. Quantifiable Impact: Showcase concrete results or case studies from past projects to substantiate the value you bring. Use metrics and success stories to build credibility.

4. Clear and Concise Messaging: Craft a succinct and compelling value proposition that leaves a lasting impression on potential clients.

5. Align with Values: Consider how your consulting aligns with your personal or business values, as clients often seek consultants who share their beliefs.

6. Continuous Improvement: Emphasize your commitment to staying at the forefront of your niche through continuous learning and keeping up with industry advancements.

7. Targeted Audience: Tailor your value proposition to specific client segments or industries to enhance relevance and effectiveness.

Remember, defining your consulting niche and value proposition is an iterative process. It requires a fusion of self-awareness, market understanding, and the willingness to adapt based on feedback and evolving industry dynamics. Embrace this journey with an open mind, and you'll discover the path that allows you to make a unique and valuable impact in the consulting world.

CHAPTER 2: DEVELOPING YOUR CONSULTING SKILL SET

Assessing Your Expertise And Skills

Assessing your expertise and skills in your new consulting business calls for a holistic and self-reflective approach, designed to reveal your strengths and identify areas for further development.

1. Deep Self-Reflection: Engage in introspection to recognize your areas of expertise and passion. Assess your knowledge, experiences, and accomplishments to gain clarity on the unique value you can offer clients.

2. Seek External Feedback: Reach out to mentors, colleagues, or clients for candid feedback on your performance and areas of strength. Embrace constructive criticism to refine your skills.

3. Evaluate Past Projects: Analyze the outcomes of previous consulting engagements. Assess the impact of your solutions on clients' businesses and identify patterns of success.

4. Conduct Skills Gap Analysis: Identify areas where you may need improvement or additional training. Focus on building competencies that align with your niche and future market demands.

5. Continuous Learning: Invest in ongoing professional development to stay abreast of industry trends and new methodologies. Attend workshops, conferences, or online courses relevant to your expertise.

6. Client Testimonials: Leverage testimonials from satisfied clients as evidence of your expertise and the value you bring. These endorsements can strengthen your credibility in the market.

7. Monitor Industry Recognition: Keep track of any awards, recognition, or certifications you've received within your consulting domain. These achievements reflect your expertise and commitment to excellence.

8. Compare Competitors: Conduct competitive analysis to understand how your expertise stacks up against other consultants in your niche. Identify areas where you excel and differentiate yourself.

9. Embrace Humility: Acknowledge that continuous improvement is an essential aspect of consulting. Embrace a growth mindset, acknowledging that there is always room for advancement.

10. Seek Challenging Projects: Take on projects that push your boundaries and require you to apply your expertise creatively. Embrace challenges as opportunities to stretch and refine your skills.

Remember, the journey of assessing your expertise is ongoing. Embrace the process with enthusiasm, welcome feedback, and remain committed to refining your skills, as it is through this commitment that you will elevate your consulting business to new heights of success.

Identifying Gaps And Areas For Development

Identifying gaps in areas for development while starting your new consulting business requires a discerning eye, a thirst for growth, and a willingness to be introspective about your venture.

1. Market Research: Conduct thorough market research to understand the current demand for consulting services in your niche. Identify gaps where clients are underserved or facing unmet needs.

2. Competitor Analysis: Analyze your competitors' strengths and weaknesses to identify areas where you can differentiate yourself and offer unique value.

3. Client Feedback: Seek feedback from potential clients, even before officially launching your business. Understand their pain points and requirements to tailor your services effectively.

4. Self-Assessment: Take an honest look at your own skills, expertise, and experiences. Identify areas where you feel less confident and might need further development.

5. Industry Trends: Stay updated with industry trends and emerging technologies in your consulting domain. Identify areas where your knowledge might need augmentation.

6. SWOT Analysis: Perform a SWOT analysis (Strengths, Weaknesses, Opportunities, Threats) of your consulting business to identify internal and external areas for improvement.

7. Professional Networks: Engage with professional networks, attend industry events, and interact with peers. This will help you gauge where you stand among your contemporaries.

8. Seek Expert Opinions: Consult with experienced mentors, advisors, or other consultants in your field. Their insights can shed light on areas you may have overlooked.

9. Pilot Projects: Consider undertaking pilot projects to test your services in a controlled environment. This will reveal potential areas for improvement before a full-scale launch.

10. Continuous Feedback Loop: Establish a feedback loop with clients throughout your consulting engagements. This will enable you to adapt and refine your approach based on real-time input.

Embrace the journey of identifying gaps and areas for development as an integral part of building a successful consulting business. Emphasize continuous learning and growth, as these elements will ultimately elevate your services, ensuring you remain dynamic and responsive to the ever-changing demands of the consulting landscape.

- Strategies for acquiring necessary knowledge and experience

Acquiring the necessary knowledge and experience for your consulting business demands a multifaceted approach that blends proactive learning, practical application, and a growth-oriented mindset.

1. Continuous Learning: Embrace a hunger for knowledge by reading books, articles, and industry publications. Attend workshops, webinars, and online courses to stay updated with the latest trends and best practices in your consulting domain.

2. Mentorship and Networking: Seek guidance from experienced mentors or join professional networks to tap into valuable insights and lessons from seasoned consultants. Build relationships with peers who can provide support and share their experiences.

3. Hands-on Experience: Gain practical experience by offering pro bono services or taking on small-scale projects initially. This allows you to apply theoretical knowledge in real-world scenarios and fine-tune your consulting skills.

4. Case Studies and Research: Conduct in-depth case studies of successful consulting projects in your niche. Analyze what worked and what didn't, drawing valuable lessons from both successes and challenges.

5. Client Feedback and Reflection: Regularly seek feedback from clients and reflect on your consulting engagements. Analyze the results and identify areas for improvement and growth.

6. Cross-Disciplinary Learning: Explore related fields and industries to broaden your perspective. This interdisciplinary approach can offer fresh insights and innovative solutions to clients' challenges.

7. Certifications and Accreditation: Consider pursuing certifications or accreditation from reputable organizations in your consulting domain. These credentials add credibility to your expertise and reassure clients of your competence.

8. Collaboration and Partnerships: Collaborate with other consultants or firms to leverage their expertise and diversify your service offerings. These partnerships can also expose you to new knowledge and working methodologies.

9. Feedback from Peers and Clients: Engage in peer review or participate in mastermind groups to gain constructive feedback from other consultants. Additionally, collect feedback from clients to understand areas where you can enhance your services.

10. Reflection and Iteration: Regularly assess your progress and growth. Celebrate your successes and embrace failures as opportunities for learning and improvement. Adopt an iterative approach to continuously evolve and refine your consulting capabilities.

By combining these strategies, you can build a solid foundation of knowledge and experience for your consulting business, setting the stage for confident and effective client engagements while remaining adaptable to the ever-evolving demands of the consulting industry.

CHAPTER 3: CRAFTING YOUR BUSINESS STRATEGY

Setting Goals And Objectives

Setting goals and objectives for your new consulting business requires a purposeful and strategic approach, encompassing clarity, focus, and adaptability.

1. Visionary Clarity: Define a clear and compelling vision for your consulting business. Envision where you want your business to be in the long term and let this vision guide your goal-setting process.

2. SMART Goals: Set Specific, Measurable, Achievable, Relevant, and Time-bound (SMART) goals. This framework ensures that your objectives are well-defined, trackable, and aligned with your overall vision.

3. Prioritize Objectives: Identify key objectives that align with your consulting niche and address critical business needs. Focus on a few essential goals to prevent spreading resources too thin.

4. Break Down Goals: Divide long-term goals into smaller milestones or short-term objectives. This makes progress more manageable and provides a sense of accomplishment as you achieve each milestone.

5. Align with Your Values: Ensure that your goals resonate with your values and align with your purpose as a consultant. This alignment fosters greater

motivation and passion for pursuing your objectives.

6. Measure Progress: Establish key performance indicators (KPIs) to measure progress towards your goals. Regularly review and assess your performance to identify areas for improvement.

7. Adaptability and Agility: Be open to adjusting your goals as the business landscape evolves. Embrace adaptability to respond to unexpected opportunities or challenges.

8. Collaborative Goal-Setting: Involve your team, if applicable, in the goal-setting process. Encourage their input and commitment, fostering a sense of ownership and shared purpose.

9. Celebrate Milestones: Celebrate achievements and milestones along the way. Recognize the efforts of yourself and your team, reinforcing a positive and motivated work environment.

10. Continuous Review: Regularly review and reassess your goals to ensure they remain relevant and aligned with your consulting business's trajectory. Make adjustments as needed to stay on course.

Remember, setting goals for your consulting business is an iterative process that demands introspection, adaptability, and a willingness to pursue excellence. Stay focused on your vision, embrace the journey, and use your goals as stepping stones toward building a successful and fulfilling consulting venture.

Conducting Market Research And Identifying Target Clients

Conducting thorough market research and identifying target clients for your new consulting business requires a strategic and data-driven approach, combining a deep understanding of your expertise with insights into the needs and preferences of potential clients.

1. Define Your Consulting Niche: Begin by clearly defining your consulting niche, identifying the specific area where you excel and can deliver significant value. A well-defined niche helps you focus your research and tailor your services to meet distinct client requirements.

2. Competitive Landscape Analysis: Analyze your competitors' offerings, strengths, and weaknesses. Identify gaps in the market where you can differentiate yourself and create a unique value proposition.

3. Client Personas: Create detailed client personas representing your ideal clients. Understand their demographics, pain points, challenges, and goals. This helps in targeting your marketing efforts effectively.

4. Surveys and Interviews: Conduct surveys or interviews with potential clients and industry experts to gather firsthand insights. These interactions provide valuable feedback and uncover unmet needs in the market.

5. Online Research: Utilize online resources like industry reports, market trends, and relevant forums to stay informed about the latest developments in your consulting domain.

6. Networking and Referrals: Build strong professional networks and leverage referrals to connect with potential clients. Engaging in networking events or online communities can lead to valuable opportunities.

7. Data Analysis: Analyze data from your website, social media, and other marketing efforts to understand audience behavior and preferences. This data-driven approach aids in refining your target client profile.

8. Industry Associations: Join industry associations or professional groups related to your consulting field. Participation in these communities opens doors to potential clients and collaboration opportunities.

9. Pilot Projects: Offer pilot projects or pro bono services to gain firsthand experience and testimonials. This helps establish credibility and builds your reputation in the market.

10. Adaptability: Be open to adjusting your target client profile based on the insights gathered from your research. Continuously refine and update your approach to match evolving market demands.

By combining these strategies, you can create a comprehensive understanding of your target clients and their needs. This knowledge will empower you to craft tailored marketing campaigns, establish meaningful connections, and position your new consulting business for success in the competitive market landscape.

Positioning Yourself Competitively In The Market

Positioning yourself competitively in the market for your new consulting business requires a thoughtful blend of showcasing your unique strengths, differentiation strategies, and delivering exceptional value to clients:

1. Leverage Your Expertise: Highlight your specialized knowledge and skills that set you apart from competitors. Demonstrate how your unique expertise can solve clients' challenges effectively.

2. Clear Value Proposition: Craft a compelling value proposition that clearly communicates the tangible benefits clients can expect from your consulting services. Focus on the outcomes you deliver rather than just the services you provide.

3. Niche Dominance: Embrace your chosen niche and become a recognized authority in that area. Position yourself as the go-to expert for clients

seeking solutions in your specific domain.

4. Case Studies and Testimonials: Showcase successful case studies and client testimonials to substantiate your track record and build credibility. Highlight the positive impact of your consulting solutions.

5. Innovation and Adaptability: Stay at the forefront of industry trends and emerging technologies. Showcase your ability to adapt and innovate to meet evolving client needs.

6. Thought Leadership: Establish yourself as a thought leader by sharing valuable insights through blogs, articles, or speaking engagements. Positioning yourself as an industry influencer boosts your credibility.

7. Client-Centric Approach: Tailor your services to address the unique needs of each client. Demonstrate a deep understanding of their challenges and offer personalized solutions.

8. Competitive Pricing: Consider your pricing strategy to be competitive while ensuring your services' value is adequately reflected. Avoid undervaluing yourself to maintain long-term sustainability.

9. Networking and Collaborations: Build strategic partnerships with other consultants or firms to expand your reach and offer complementary services. Collaborations can enhance your service offerings.

10. Exceptional Customer Service: Provide outstanding customer service to nurture lasting relationships with clients. Satisfied clients are more likely to refer others and contribute to your reputation.

By implementing these strategies, you position your new consulting business as a sought-after and competitive player in the market. Emphasize your expertise, value proposition, and client-centric approach to attract clients, foster loyalty, and establish a strong foothold in the industry.

* * *

CHAPTER 4: BUILDING YOUR BRAND

Creating A Compelling Personal Brand

Creating a compelling personal brand for your new consulting business requires a deliberate and authentic approach, showcasing your expertise, values, and unique personality to establish a strong and memorable identity:

1. Define Your Brand Identity: Begin by defining your brand's core values, mission, and vision. This foundation will guide every aspect of your personal brand and ensure consistency in your messaging.

2. Identify Your Unique Selling Points: Identify what sets you apart from other consultants in your niche. Highlight your expertise, experience, and distinctive approach that clients can't find elsewhere.

3. Craft Your Brand Story: Share your professional journey and the reasons that led you to start your consulting business. Create a narrative that connects with your target audience on a personal level.

4. Consistent Online Presence: Build a professional website and optimize your social media profiles to reflect your brand identity consistently. Use professional headshots, brand colors, and a cohesive tone of voice.

5. Thought Leadership Content: Establish yourself as a thought leader in your consulting domain by creating valuable and insightful content. Share

expertise through blog posts, articles, videos, or podcast episodes.

6. Engage in Social Media: Interact with your audience on social media platforms regularly. Respond to comments, share industry news, and participate in relevant discussions to build a community around your brand.

7. Networking and Collaborations: Attend industry events, webinars, and networking sessions to connect with peers and potential clients. Collaborate with other professionals to expand your brand's reach.

8. Client Testimonials and Case Studies: Display client testimonials and success stories on your website to build trust and demonstrate your consulting impact.

9. Webinars and Speaking Engagements: Host webinars or participate in speaking engagements to showcase your expertise and reach a broader audience.

10. Authenticity and Transparency: Be genuine and transparent in your interactions. Clients value authenticity, and it helps establish credibility and trust in your brand.

Remember, a compelling personal brand is more than just visual elements; it embodies your values, expertise, and the positive impact you bring to clients. Stay true to your authentic self while positioning yourself as an industry expert, and your personal brand will resonate with your target audience, paving the way for long-term success in your consulting business.

Crafting A Powerful Mission And Vision Statement

Crafting a powerful mission and vision statement for your consulting business involves a thoughtful process of introspection, purposeful messaging, and forward-looking aspirations:

Mission Statement:

1. Core Purpose: Begin by defining the fundamental reason your consulting business exists. Clarify the primary purpose of your services and the positive impact you aim to make on clients' businesses or lives.

2. Target Audience: Clearly identify your target clients and the specific challenges you aim to address. Tailor your mission to resonate with their needs and aspirations.

3. Unique Approach: Highlight the distinctive methodologies, values, or principles that set your consulting services apart. Emphasize what makes your approach different and impactful.

4. Conciseness: Keep your mission statement concise and clear. Aim to convey the essence of your consulting purpose in a few powerful sentences.

Vision Statement:

1. Future Aspirations: Envision the future trajectory of your consulting business. Paint a compelling picture of what you aim to achieve in the long term and the positive change you seek to bring.

2. Inspiring Language: Use inspiring and evocative language that ignites passion and excitement in both your team and clients. Communicate the ambitious goals you strive to reach.

3. Alignment with Values: Ensure your vision statement aligns with your core values and overarching objectives. It should encapsulate your ideals and represent the legacy you want to leave.

4. Realistic Yet Ambitious: Strike a balance between ambition and feasibility. Your vision should be aspirational but grounded in a sense of practicality and attainability.

5. Evoking Emotion: Create an emotional connection with your stakeholders by conveying a vision that inspires and motivates them to be a part of your journey.

Remember, your mission and vision statements serve as guiding beacons for your consulting business. They should encapsulate your unique identity, aspirations, and commitment to creating a meaningful impact. Take the time to craft statements that resonate deeply with you and your target audience, as they will shape the direction and purpose of your consulting business for years to come.

Developing A Strong Online Presence

Developing a strong online presence for your new consulting business requires a strategic and cohesive approach, combining various digital elements to build credibility, reach your target audience, and showcase your expertise:

1. Professional Website: Create a well-designed, user-friendly website that reflects your brand identity and showcases your consulting services. Ensure it includes essential information such as your mission, services, testimonials, and contact details.

2. Content Marketing: Publish valuable and insightful content on your website's blog. Share expertise, industry trends, and solutions to address clients' challenges. Consistency in content creation establishes you as a thought leader and boosts your search engine rankings.

3. Search Engine Optimization (SEO): Optimize your website with relevant keywords and metadata to improve its visibility on search engines. This helps potential clients find you when searching for consulting services in your niche.

4. Social Media Presence: Choose platforms relevant to your target audience and engage regularly. Share your content, participate in discussions, and build a community around your brand. Social media is a powerful tool for connecting and building relationships.

5. LinkedIn Engagement: Leverage LinkedIn to establish your professional credibility. Share updates, publish articles, and actively participate in industry groups to expand your network and attract potential clients.

6. Email Marketing: Build an email list and nurture leads with valuable content, updates, and offers. Email marketing is a personal way to stay connected with your audience and showcase your expertise.

7. Webinars and Online Events: Host webinars, workshops, or online events to share your knowledge and interact with your target audience. This strengthens your brand authority and allows you to engage with potential clients directly.

8. Client Testimonials and Case Studies: Display client testimonials and success stories on your website. These social proofs build trust and credibility, encouraging potential clients to choose your consulting services.

9. Online Partnerships and Collaborations: Collaborate with other professionals or influencers in your industry. Joint projects or guest appearances on each other's platforms can expand your reach and attract new clients.

10. Monitor and Analyze: Regularly monitor your online presence, analyze website traffic, and track engagement metrics. Use the data to refine your strategies and improve your digital performance.

Consistency, authenticity, and providing value are crucial when developing your online presence. By strategically combining these digital elements, you can establish a robust online presence that attracts your target audience, showcases your expertise, and

*positions your new consulting business for long-term success in the
digital landscape.*

* * *

CHAPTER 5: ESTABLISHING YOUR CONSULTING BUSINESS

Choosing A Legal Structure For Your Business

Choosing the right legal structure for your consulting business is a critical decision that impacts your liability, taxes, and overall business operations. To ensure you make an informed choice:

1. Research and Understanding: Conduct thorough research on different legal structures, such as sole proprietorship, partnership, LLC, or corporation. Understand the implications, advantages, and disadvantages of each option.

2. Business Goals: Align the legal structure with your long-term business goals. Consider factors like scalability, expansion plans, and the potential for adding partners or investors.

3. Liability Protection: Evaluate the level of personal liability you're comfortable with. Some structures offer limited liability protection, safeguarding your personal assets from business debts and lawsuits.

4. Tax Considerations: Analyze the tax implications of each legal structure. Some structures provide tax benefits, while others might subject you to self-employment taxes or corporate taxes.

5. Cost and Complexity: Assess the setup costs, ongoing compliance requirements, and administrative complexity associated with each structure. Choose one that aligns with your resources and operational preferences.

6. Flexibility: Consider the flexibility each legal structure offers in terms of management, decision-making, and ownership.

7. Consult Legal and Financial Professionals: Seek advice from legal and financial advisors to get personalized insights into how each structure aligns with your specific business needs and financial situation.

8. Future Changes: Anticipate potential changes in your business over time. Select a legal structure that accommodates growth and any future changes in ownership or operations.

9. Industry Regulations: Be aware of any specific legal requirements or regulations that might apply to your consulting niche. Ensure your chosen legal structure complies with industry-specific rules.

10. Risk Analysis: Perform a risk analysis to identify potential vulnerabilities and liabilities associated with each legal structure. Opt for the one that offers the best balance between risk management and operational flexibility.

Ultimately, take your time in deciding the legal structure for your consulting business. Weigh the pros and cons of each option in light of your unique circumstances, aspirations, and risk tolerance. This thoughtful approach will help you choose the legal structure that best supports the success and longevity of your consulting venture.

Registering Your Business And Acquiring Necessary Licenses

Registering your consulting business and acquiring necessary licenses require careful adherence to legal requirements and government regulations. Follow these steps to ensure a smooth and compliant process:

1. Business Structure Selection: Choose the legal structure that aligns with your business goals and provides the desired level of liability protection. Options include sole proprietorship, partnership, LLC, or corporation.

2. Business Name Registration: Select a unique and memorable name for your consulting business. Check its availability and register it with the appropriate government agency in your region.

3. Obtain Employer Identification Number (EIN): If applicable to your business structure or if you plan to hire employees, acquire an EIN from the IRS. This nine-digit number is used for tax purposes.

4. Business Permits and Licenses: Research and obtain the necessary business permits and licenses required for your consulting services. Requirements vary based on your location, industry, and services provided.

5. Local Business Regulations: Comply with local business regulations, zoning laws, and any specific industry requirements that may apply to your consulting niche.

6. State Registration: Register your consulting business with the state's business authority. This step formalizes your business and ensures legal compliance.

7. Taxation Registration: Register for federal, state, and local taxes, including sales tax if applicable. Consult with a tax professional to understand your tax obligations and how to handle tax filings.

8. Insurance Coverage: Consider obtaining professional liability insurance to protect your business from potential claims or lawsuits related to your consulting services.

9. Business Bank Account: Open a separate business bank account to keep your personal and business finances distinct. This facilitates accurate financial record-keeping and simplifies tax reporting.

10. Consult Legal and Financial Advisors: Seek guidance from legal and financial professionals to navigate the registration and licensing process efficiently. They can help you understand the specific requirements based on your business structure and location.

Remember, compliance with legal regulations is crucial for the success and credibility of your consulting business. By meticulously completing the necessary registrations and acquiring the appropriate licenses, you set the foundation for a well-structured and law-abiding venture, positioning your business for growth and longevity in the consulting industry.

Setting Up Financial Systems And Managing Cash Flow

Setting up robust financial systems and managing cash flow effectively are vital aspects of running a successful consulting business. Follow these steps to establish sound financial practices:

1. Separate Business and Personal Finances: Open a dedicated business bank account to ensure clear separation between personal and business finances. This simplifies tracking income and expenses and helps with tax reporting.

2. Financial Software: Invest in reliable accounting software to manage your finances efficiently. Automate invoicing, expense tracking, and financial reporting to save time and minimize errors.

3. Budgeting: Create a detailed budget outlining your projected income and expenses. Regularly review and adjust the budget to maintain financial stability and avoid overspending.

4. Cash Flow Forecasting: Forecast your cash flow to anticipate potential fluctuations and plan for periods of low income. This enables you to make informed decisions and ensure you have sufficient funds to cover expenses.

5. Invoicing and Payment Terms: Establish clear invoicing practices with professional invoices and clearly defined payment terms. Encourage prompt payments to maintain steady cash flow.

6. Payment Follow-Up: Implement a system to follow up on outstanding payments. Be proactive in reminding clients about upcoming due dates and addressing late payments promptly.

7. Expense Management: Monitor expenses closely and look for opportunities to cut unnecessary costs. Consider negotiating with vendors and suppliers to obtain favorable terms.

8. Emergency Fund: Build an emergency fund to cover unexpected expenses or revenue gaps. Having a financial safety net provides peace of mind during challenging times.

9. Tax Planning: Work with a tax professional to understand your tax obligations and develop a tax plan. Set aside funds for taxes regularly to avoid surprises during tax season.

10. Regular Financial Review: Conduct regular financial reviews to assess your business's financial health. Analyze profit margins, identify trends, and use data to make informed financial decisions.

By implementing these financial practices, you can establish a strong foundation for your consulting business. Proper financial systems and cash flow management contribute to financial stability and pave the way for long-term success and growth in your consulting venture.

CHAPTER 6: MARKETING AND CLIENT ACQUISITION

Designing A Marketing Plan And Identifying Effective Marketing Channels

Designing an effective marketing plan and identifying suitable marketing channels for your new consulting business requires a strategic and customer-centric approach. Follow these steps to create a compelling marketing strategy:

1. Know Your Target Audience: Conduct thorough market research to understand your ideal clients' needs, pain points, and preferences. This knowledge forms the foundation of your marketing plan.

2. Craft a Clear Value Proposition: Develop a compelling value proposition that communicates the unique benefits your consulting services offer. Clearly articulate how you can solve clients' problems and address their specific challenges.

3. Set Clear Marketing Goals: Define specific and measurable marketing goals aligned with your business objectives. Whether it's increasing brand awareness, generating leads, or expanding your client base, clarity in your goals is essential.

4. Choose Relevant Marketing Channels: Based on your target audience's preferences and behavior, select marketing channels that resonate with them. This may include content marketing, social media, email campaigns, networking events, or webinars.

5. Content Marketing Strategy: Create valuable and informative content that positions you as an industry expert. Utilize blog posts, articles, videos, or podcasts to share insights and engage your audience.

6. Leverage Social Media: Use social media platforms that align with your target audience to share your expertise, interact with potential clients, and build brand awareness.

7. Email Marketing: Build an email list and nurture leads with relevant content and personalized communication. Email marketing is an effective way to establish and maintain client relationships.

8. Networking and Partnerships: Attend industry events, join professional associations, and collaborate with other consultants or firms to expand your network and gain referrals.

9. Client Testimonials and Case Studies: Showcase satisfied clients' testimonials and success stories on your website and social media. Positive reviews build trust and credibility.

10. Track and Analyze Results: Monitor the performance of your marketing efforts regularly. Use analytics to measure the effectiveness of each channel and adjust your strategies based on data-driven insights.

Remember, an effective marketing plan is adaptable and evolves as your consulting business grows. Continuously listen to your clients' feedback, stay up-to-date with industry trends, and be open to refining your marketing strategies to ensure your consulting business thrives in a competitive market.

Building A Network And Establishing Relationships With Potential Clients

Building a strong network and establishing meaningful relationships with potential clients requires a combination of authenticity, genuine interest, and a value-driven approach. Follow these steps to cultivate a valuable network for your consulting business:

1. Identify Target Clients: Clearly define your target audience and focus on building relationships with individuals and businesses that align with your consulting niche and can benefit from your expertise.

2. Attend Industry Events: Participate in conferences, seminars, workshops, and networking events related to your consulting domain. These gatherings offer valuable opportunities to connect with potential clients and industry peers.

3. Utilize Social Media: Engage with your target audience on social media platforms relevant to your industry. Share valuable content, interact with comments, and respond to direct messages to build rapport.

4. Join Professional Associations: Become a member of industry-specific professional associations. Participate in discussions, contribute insights, and collaborate with like-minded professionals.

5. Offer Value First: Be generous with your expertise. Share valuable insights through blog posts, webinars, or free resources to showcase your knowledge and establish credibility.

6. Personalized Outreach: Reach out to potential clients individually with personalized messages. Avoid generic, sales-focused pitches and instead, show a genuine interest in their business and challenges.

7. Attend Meetups and Workshops: Participate in local meetups, workshops, and community events to build connections with potential clients in your

area.

8. Follow Up Consistently: After initial interactions, follow up with potential clients to nurture relationships. Be consistent in your communication without being pushy.

9. Offer Pro Bono Services: Consider offering pro bono services or short consultations as a way to demonstrate your value and build trust with potential clients.

10. Stay Curious and Learn: Continuously educate yourself about your industry and stay informed about current trends and challenges. Being well-informed allows you to engage in meaningful conversations with potential clients.

Remember, building a network and establishing relationships with potential clients is not solely about selling your services. Instead, focus on creating authentic connections, offering value, and demonstrating how your consulting expertise can genuinely benefit them. By fostering meaningful relationships, you'll position yourself as a trusted advisor and increase the likelihood of attracting clients who are eager to work with you.

Developing A Sales Strategy And Closing Deals

The art of closing deals and developing a successful sales strategy for your new consulting business requires a delicate blend of persuasive finesse, client-centric focus, and the tenacity of a guiding compass, navigating you through the ever-changing currents of the market. Follow these original steps to master the art of deal closure:

1. Embrace Authentic Empathy: Infuse genuine empathy into your interactions with potential clients. Understanding their needs and aspirations allows you to tailor your solutions with heartfelt precision.

2. Consultative Storytelling: Weave the power of storytelling into your sales process. Artfully narrate success stories, painting vivid images of how your consulting solutions have transformed businesses, capturing clients' imagination.

3. Adaptive Listening: Develop the art of adaptive listening, intuitively attuning yourself to clients' verbal and non-verbal cues. This skillful dance of receptiveness enables you to address concerns and position yourself as a trusted confidant.

4. Navigate Objections with Grace: Embrace objections as stepping stones rather than obstacles. With grace and insightful finesse, navigate through clients' concerns, turning objections into opportunities to deepen rapport.

5. Holistic Problem-Solving: Embrace a holistic problem-solving approach. Beyond selling services, become a strategic partner in crafting comprehensive solutions tailored to clients' unique needs.

6. Incorporate Agile Flexibility: Adapt your sales strategy with agile flexibility, attuned to the ever-shifting tides of the market. Embrace a dynamic approach that navigates uncertainties while keeping your vision clear.

7. Collaborative Ideation: Cultivate a collaborative atmosphere during negotiations. Engage clients in ideation, co-creating visions of success that foster a sense of ownership in the process.

8. Value Co-Creation: Position yourself as a value co-creator, articulating how your consulting acumen synergizes with clients' aspirations to unlock unparalleled potential.

9. Timely Follow-Up: Extend thoughtful and timely follow-ups that exemplify your commitment. Demonstrate attentiveness in nurturing the

seeds of potential into flourishing partnerships.
10. Leverage Referral Ecosystems: Cultivate an organic referral ecosystem by exceeding clients' expectations. Harness the potency of word-of-mouth advocacy, propelling your consulting business toward boundless growth.

By harmonizing these original strategies, you will craft a sales strategy that resonates deeply with potential clients, igniting a spark of trust and igniting a passionate drive for mutually transformative partnerships. Let the symphony of authenticity, creativity, and empathy orchestrate your journey towards successful deal closure and a flourishing consulting enterprise.

* * *

CHAPTER 7: DELIVERING EXCEPTIONAL CONSULTING SERVICES

Understanding Client Needs And Expectations

The best way to understand client needs and expectations for your consulting business is through active listening, open communication, and a client-centric approach. Follow these steps to gain a deep understanding of your clients' requirements:

1. Initial Consultation: Begin with an in-depth initial consultation with potential clients. Encourage them to express their goals, challenges, and expectations openly.

2. Ask Thoughtful Questions: Pose thoughtful and probing questions during meetings to delve into the specifics of their needs. Show genuine curiosity and a desire to comprehend their unique situation.

3. Listen Actively: Practice active listening during conversations with clients. Pay attention to their words, tone, and body language to grasp the nuances of their requirements.

4. Clarify and Recap: Repeat and clarify clients' statements to ensure a shared understanding. Recap key points to demonstrate that you value their input.

5. Client Surveys: Conduct client surveys or feedback forms after engagements to gather comprehensive insights into their experiences and expectations.

6. Follow-Up Calls: Schedule follow-up calls to check on clients' progress and address any evolving needs. This demonstrates your commitment to their success.

7. Industry Research: Keep abreast of industry trends and challenges relevant to your clients. Understanding their market context helps you align your services more effectively.

8. Engage with Decision-Makers: If possible, interact directly with the decision-makers in the client's organization. This ensures you have a clear understanding of their strategic objectives.

9. Stay Curious: Maintain a continuous learning mindset. Be curious about clients' evolving needs, as industries and businesses are dynamic.

10. Feedback and Adaptation: Encourage clients to provide feedback on your services throughout the engagement. Use this feedback to adapt and refine your approach.

Understanding client needs and expectations requires ongoing dedication and active engagement. By being attentive, responsive, and client-focused, you can develop deep insights into their requirements and deliver solutions that exceed their expectations. This client-centric approach fosters long-term relationships, repeat business, and positive referrals, solidifying your consulting business's reputation for excellence.

Designing Tailored Solutions And Value Propositions

Designing tailored solutions and value propositions for your consulting business demands an intricate tapestry of empathetic understanding, creative innovation, and client collaboration. Follow these original steps to craft compelling and personalized offerings:

1. Deep Empathy with Clients: Immerse yourself in your clients' world, seeking to understand their aspirations, challenges, and unique perspectives. Empathy forms the foundation for personalized solutions.

2. Client-Centric Discovery: Conduct comprehensive discovery sessions with clients, delving into the intricacies of their businesses or projects. Unearth their specific pain points and untapped opportunities.

3. Customization and Flexibility: Embrace the art of customization, tailoring your services to address each client's distinct needs. Offer flexible options that accommodate varying budgets and preferences.

4. Co-Creation with Clients: Foster a collaborative atmosphere where clients actively participate in shaping solutions. Engage in co-creation, harnessing the power of shared insights and ideas.

5. Leverage Your Expertise: Weave your unique expertise and strengths into the fabric of each solution. Showcase how your consulting acumen complements clients' goals.

6. Innovative Problem-Solving: Cultivate a culture of innovative problem-solving. Embrace creativity to design solutions that push boundaries and unlock unforeseen possibilities.

7. Quantifiable Value: Articulate the quantifiable value your solutions bring to clients. Clearly demonstrate how your services yield tangible and measurable outcomes.

8. Continuous Refinement: Treat each solution as an evolving masterpiece. Stay receptive to client feedback and continuously refine your offerings to surpass expectations.

9. Adapt to Evolving Needs: Recognize that clients' needs may evolve over time. Remain adaptable, ready to adjust your approach to meet changing requirements.

10. Testimonials and Case Studies: Showcase the success stories of previous clients through testimonials and case studies. These real-world examples underscore the effectiveness of your tailored solutions.

By weaving together the threads of empathy, creativity, and client collaboration, you create a mosaic of personalized solutions and value propositions that resonate profoundly with your clients. This dedication to tailored excellence cements your reputation as a consulting partner who crafts bespoke solutions, uniquely equipped to unlock the potential of every client's journey to success.

Building Client Relationships And Fostering Long-Term Partnerships

Building lasting client relationships and fostering enduring partnerships with your consulting business requires the delicate art of trust-building, authentic rapport, and unwavering dedication. Follow these original steps to cultivate a strong foundation for enduring connections:

1. Trust as the Keystone: Establish trust as the cornerstone of your relationships. Demonstrate reliability, transparency, and ethical conduct in every interaction with clients.

2. Listen with Intention: Embrace the power of attentive listening. Understand clients' needs, aspirations, and concerns to tailor solutions that resonate with their unique visions.

3. Anticipate and Exceed Expectations: Go beyond meeting expectations by anticipating clients' needs and proactively delivering exceptional value. Surpassing expectations nurtures loyalty.

4. Timely Responsiveness: Prioritize timely responsiveness to clients' inquiries and concerns. Prompt communication reflects your commitment to their success.

5. Consistency in Communication: Maintain regular and meaningful communication, even after the initial engagement. Stay engaged with updates, industry insights, and thoughtful follow-ups.

6. Personalization Matters: Customize your approach for each client, acknowledging their individual preferences and business dynamics. Personalization fosters a deeper connection.

7. Celebrate Milestones Together: Acknowledge achievements and milestones in clients' journeys. Celebrating successes strengthens the bond and reaffirms your role as a valuable partner.

8. Thoughtful Gestures: Incorporate thoughtful gestures into your interactions. Whether a handwritten note or a personalized recommendation, small acts leave a lasting impact.

9. Nurture Ongoing Learning: Continuously expand your expertise to better serve clients. Be a lifelong learner, offering innovative insights and solutions.

10. Embrace a Long-Term Perspective: Cultivate relationships with a long-term perspective in mind. View each engagement as a stepping stone towards enduring partnerships.

By weaving trust, personalized care, and a commitment to surpassing expectations, you sow the seeds of enduring client relationships. Nourished by authenticity and dedication, these relationships blossom into vibrant partnerships that stand the test of time. As you journey together, these connections become the true testament to your consulting business's impact and the legacy of your transformative contributions to clients' success.

* * *

CHAPTER 8: MANAGING OPERATIONS AND SCALING

Efficient Project Management And Resource Allocation

Utilizing efficient project management and resource allocation is crucial for maximizing productivity and delivering exceptional results in your consulting business. Follow these steps to optimize your project management practices and resource allocation:

1. Define Clear Project Objectives: Start each project with well-defined objectives, scope, and deliverables. Clearly communicate these to your team and clients to align everyone's focus.

2. Use Project Management Tools: Employ project management software to streamline workflows, track progress, and manage tasks efficiently. These tools facilitate collaboration and keep everyone on the same page.

3. Create Realistic Timelines: Set realistic timelines for each project phase, considering potential challenges and dependencies. Avoid over-promising and underestimating the time required for tasks.

4. Allocate Resources Wisely: Identify the right resources (human, financial, and technological) required for each project. Ensure that your team members have the necessary skills and expertise to handle their roles effectively.

5. Effective Communication: Establish open and transparent communication channels among team members and clients. Regularly update stakeholders on progress, milestones, and potential roadblocks.

6. Risk Management: Proactively identify project risks and develop contingency plans. Mitigate potential issues before they escalate, minimizing disruptions to project timelines.

7. Prioritize Tasks: Focus on high-priority tasks and allocate resources accordingly. This prevents unnecessary delays and ensures that critical milestones are achieved on time.

8. Empower Your Team: Encourage a culture of autonomy and ownership among your team members. Empowered individuals are more likely to take ownership of their tasks and contribute to project success.

9. Continuous Improvement: Regularly evaluate project management processes and resource allocation. Seek feedback from team members and clients to identify areas for improvement.

10. Track and Analyze Performance: Monitor project performance metrics to assess efficiency and identify opportunities for optimization. Data-driven insights help refine future resource allocation decisions.

Efficient project management and resource allocation are key drivers of success in the consulting business. By adopting organized practices, empowering your team, and prioritizing client needs, you optimize your operations, deliver projects more effectively, and build a reputation for excellence in your industry.

Developing Systems For Efficient Operations

Developing systems for efficient operations in your consulting business entails orchestrating a symphony of meticulous planning, streamlined processes, and harmonious collaboration. Follow these original steps to create a well-tuned operation:

1. Standardize Workflows: Define clear and standardized workflows for common tasks in your consulting processes. Document these procedures to ensure consistency and ease of execution.

2. Leverage Technology: Embrace technology solutions that streamline operations, such as project management software, CRM systems, and automation tools. Harness the power of digitalization for enhanced efficiency.

3. Empower Your Team: Foster a culture of ownership and empowerment among your team members. Encourage them to take initiative and contribute innovative ideas to improve operations.

4. Continuous Training: Invest in ongoing training and professional development for your team. Keep them updated with industry best practices and new skills to enhance their performance.

5. Client Onboarding Process: Create a structured and welcoming client onboarding process. This ensures a smooth transition from prospect to engaged client, setting the stage for successful collaborations.

6. Streamlined Communication: Establish efficient communication channels, both internally and externally. Implement regular check-ins and status updates to keep everyone informed and aligned.

7. Data-Driven Decision Making: Utilize data analytics to make informed business decisions. Analyzing performance metrics and key indicators helps identify areas for improvement.

8. Cross-Functional Collaboration: Encourage cross-functional collaboration to leverage diverse expertise within your team. This

collaboration sparks creativity and leads to comprehensive solutions.

9. Client Feedback Loop: Create a feedback loop with clients to gather insights on their experience and satisfaction. Use this feedback to refine and optimize your operations.

10. Monitor and Adapt: Continuously monitor the efficiency of your systems and be open to adapting them as your business evolves. Flexibility and adaptability are essential for sustained success.

Efficient operations are the backbone of a successful consulting business. By developing systems that prioritize consistency, innovation, and client-centricity, you create a harmonious environment where your team thrives and clients experience exceptional service. Embrace the journey of continuous improvement, and your consulting business will resonate as a well-tuned symphony, leaving a lasting impression on both clients and the industry at large.

Strategies For Scaling Your Consulting Business

Scaling your consulting business requires a strategic approach that encompasses various aspects of your operations and client acquisition. Here are some strategies to effectively scale your consulting business:

1. Leverage Your Expertise: Focus on your core strengths and expertise. Specializing in a niche allows you to establish yourself as an industry authority, attracting more clients seeking your specific services.

2. Build a Strong Team: As your business grows, invest in building a skilled and motivated team. Surround yourself with talented individuals who complement your abilities and share your vision.

3. Streamline Processes: Optimize your internal processes to improve efficiency and productivity. Automation, standardization, and clear workflows reduce manual tasks, allowing you to handle more clients effectively.

4. Diversify Revenue Streams: Explore additional revenue streams that align with your consulting business. This may include offering online courses, publishing books, or creating digital products related to your expertise.

5. Expand Client Base: Implement targeted marketing strategies to reach a broader audience. Utilize digital marketing, content creation, social media, and networking to attract new clients.

6. Form Strategic Partnerships: Collaborate with complementary businesses or other consultants to extend your reach and offer comprehensive solutions. Strategic partnerships can lead to new opportunities and clients.

7. Deliver Exceptional Service: Prioritize delivering outstanding service to your clients. Satisfied clients are more likely to provide referrals and positive testimonials, which contribute to your business growth.

8. Invest in Marketing: Allocate resources to marketing initiatives that yield the best results. Continuously measure the effectiveness of marketing efforts and adapt strategies based on data.

9. Scalable Pricing Model: Create scalable pricing models that accommodate different client needs and budgets. Consider offering retainer packages or project-based options to attract a diverse clientele.

10. Embrace Technology: Embrace technology to streamline communication, project management, and client interactions. Utilize CRM systems, project management tools, and online collaboration platforms.

11. Expand Geographically: Consider expanding your consulting services to new geographic regions or international markets. Technology enables you

to work with clients worldwide.

12. Invest in Your Brand: Build a strong and reputable brand. Invest in your website, branding, and client testimonials to enhance your credibility and attract larger clients.

Remember, scaling a consulting business is a gradual process that requires careful planning and execution. Focus on sustainable growth, continuous improvement, and staying true to your core values. By implementing these strategies, you can position your consulting business for steady expansion and long-term success.

* * *

CHAPTER 9: OVERCOMING CHALLENGES AND OBSTACLES

Identifying Common Challenges In Consulting And How To Overcome Them

Identifying and overcoming common challenges in consulting requires a discerning eye, strategic problem-solving, and an unwavering commitment to excellence. Here's how to navigate these obstacles with originality:

1. Unclear Scope and Expectations: Clearly define the scope of each project and set realistic expectations with clients from the outset. Maintain open communication and manage any scope changes promptly.

2. Time Management Pressures: Prioritize tasks effectively and delegate when necessary. Set realistic timelines and avoid overcommitting. Embrace time-tracking tools to optimize your productivity.

3. Client Communication: Establish strong client communication channels. Actively listen to their needs and concerns, respond promptly, and offer regular updates to foster transparent collaboration.

4. Scope Creep: Stay vigilant against scope creep during projects. Clearly document any changes in scope and seek approval before proceeding.

5. Competitive Market: Set yourself apart in a competitive market by emphasizing your unique value proposition, specialized expertise, and exceptional service delivery.

6. Managing Client Expectations: Ensure that clients have a clear understanding of the consulting process and potential outcomes. Provide realistic timelines and be transparent about possible challenges.

7. Resistance to Change: Anticipate and address resistance to change within client organizations. Foster a culture of openness and support during the implementation of your consulting solutions.

8. Balancing Workload: Strike a balance between client work and business development efforts. Allocate time for marketing, networking, and continuous learning to sustain growth.

9. Handling Rejections: Embrace rejection as an opportunity for growth. Learn from each experience, adapt your approach, and maintain confidence in your value proposition.

10. Continual Learning: Stay at the forefront of industry trends and best practices. Invest in continuous learning and professional development to enhance your consulting capabilities.

11. Client Diversity: Embrace the diversity of client needs and backgrounds. Tailor your approach to address the unique challenges of each client while maintaining a consistent level of excellence.

12. Adapting to New Technologies: Embrace technology advancements that can enhance your consulting processes. Incorporate innovative tools and platforms to improve efficiency and client outcomes.

By embracing challenges as opportunities for growth and leveraging your originality in addressing them, you cultivate a reputation for resilience and ingenuity in the consulting realm. Armed with strategic foresight and an unwavering commitment to surpassing obstacles, you position your consulting business for long-term success and the steadfast loyalty of satisfied clients.

Handling Difficult Clients And Managing Conflicts

Handling difficult clients and managing conflicts in your consulting business requires a delicate balance of empathy, assertiveness, and effective communication. Approach these situations with originality and finesse using these steps:

1. Active Listening and Empathy: Start by actively listening to your clients' concerns and frustrations. Show genuine empathy and validate their feelings, even if you disagree with their perspective.

2. Focus on Solutions: Shift the focus from the problem to finding solutions. Collaboratively explore ways to address the issues and align on a path forward that benefits both parties.

3. Set Clear Boundaries: Establish clear boundaries regarding expectations, communication channels, and project scope. Communicate these boundaries in a professional and assertive manner.

4. Maintain Professionalism: Remain professional and composed, even in challenging situations. Avoid taking things personally and respond with a calm and objective demeanor.

5. Address Concerns Proactively: Anticipate potential conflicts and address concerns proactively. Openly discuss any potential challenges and agree on contingency plans if needed.

6. Offer Alternatives: Propose alternative approaches or modifications to meet the client's needs while staying true to your consulting expertise and

principles.

7. Delegate Conflicts Appropriately: If emotions are running high, consider delegating the conflict resolution to a neutral third party within your team or involve a mediator if necessary.

8. Document Everything: Keep a detailed record of all client interactions, decisions, and agreements. This documentation provides clarity and helps resolve any misunderstandings later on.

9. Seek Common Ground: Look for common ground and shared objectives with the client. Emphasize your shared commitment to achieving success, reinforcing a collaborative atmosphere.

10. Learning from Conflicts: After resolving conflicts, reflect on the experience and learn from it. Use the insights gained to improve client communication and prevent similar conflicts in the future.

By navigating difficult client situations with authenticity and finesse, you can transform challenging moments into opportunities for strengthened relationships and mutual growth. The ability to effectively manage conflicts fosters a reputation for professionalism and resilience, positioning your consulting business as a trusted partner, even in the face of adversity.

Building Resilience And Maintaining Motivation

Becoming more resilient and maintaining motivation in your consulting business requires a combination of self-awareness, positive mindset, and proactive strategies.

Follow these steps to build resilience and stay motivated:

1. Cultivate a Growth Mindset: Embrace challenges as opportunities for learning and growth. View setbacks as stepping stones towards improvement rather than insurmountable obstacles.

2. Set Realistic Goals: Establish achievable and meaningful goals for your consulting business. Break them down into smaller milestones to celebrate progress along the way.

3. Celebrate Successes: Acknowledge and celebrate your achievements, no matter how small. Recognizing your progress boosts motivation and reinforces your confidence.

4. Practice Self-Care: Take care of your physical and mental well-being. Prioritize regular exercise, sufficient rest, and stress-reducing activities to stay resilient and maintain motivation.

5. Seek Supportive Networks: Surround yourself with supportive peers, mentors, or like-minded professionals. Engage in networking to share experiences, gain insights, and find encouragement.

6. Manage Stress Effectively: Develop coping mechanisms to handle stress constructively. This may include mindfulness practices, deep breathing exercises, or engaging in hobbies.

7. Learn from Setbacks: Analyze setbacks and learn from them. Use the lessons to adapt your approach and refine your strategies for future challenges.

8. Break Tasks into Manageable Steps: Overcome feelings of overwhelm by breaking larger tasks into smaller, manageable steps. Tackling one step at a time fosters a sense of progress and accomplishment.

9. Stay Curious and Open-Minded: Maintain curiosity and an open mind. Embrace new ideas, seek feedback, and be willing to explore alternative approaches.

10. Visualize Success: Visualize your desired outcomes and imagine yourself achieving your goals. Visualization can boost motivation and reinforce your belief in your abilities.

11. Limit Negative Self-Talk: Challenge negative self-talk and replace it with positive affirmations. Develop a habit of self-encouragement and self-compassion.

12. Reflect on Your Purpose: Reconnect with your purpose and the passion that drives your consulting business. Understanding the "why" behind your work keeps you motivated during challenging times.

By cultivating resilience and maintaining motivation, you strengthen your ability to navigate the highs and lows of running a consulting business. Embrace the journey as an opportunity for growth, and let your determination and passion guide you towards sustained success and fulfillment in your consulting endeavors.

* * *

CHAPTER 10: ETHICAL CONSIDERATIONS AND PROFESSIONAL CONDUCT

Understanding Ethical Guidelines For Consultants

The best way to understand ethical guidelines for consultants is to immerse yourself in a thoughtful exploration of industry standards, professional codes of conduct, and ethical principles that form the moral compass of your consulting practice. Follow these original steps to gain a comprehensive understanding:

1. Explore Professional Associations: Investigate ethical guidelines provided by reputable consulting professional associations specific to your industry. These associations often offer comprehensive codes of conduct that serve as ethical beacons.

2. Study Ethical Case Studies: Engage in the examination of real-life ethical case studies faced by consultants. Analyze the decisions made and their impact on clients and stakeholders, drawing valuable insights from each scenario.

3. Seek Mentorship and Guidance: Connect with experienced consultants or mentors who embody ethical practices. Their wisdom and experiences can provide invaluable guidance and help you navigate ethical challenges.

4. Review Industry Regulations: Familiarize yourself with industry-specific regulations and legal requirements. Understanding the legal framework helps you align ethical practices with legal obligations.

5. Engage in Ethical Dialogues: Participate in ethical dialogues and discussions with fellow consultants or thought leaders. Sharing diverse perspectives enriches your ethical perspective.

6. Consult Ethics Experts: Seek advice from ethicists or professionals specializing in ethics to deepen your understanding. Their expertise can provide valuable insights into ethical dilemmas.

7. Consider Client Perspectives: Reflect on the ethical expectations and needs of your clients. Understanding their values and concerns allows you to align your practices accordingly.

8. Adopt a Reflective Approach: Continuously reflect on your own ethical decision-making process. Identify areas for improvement and strive for ethical excellence.

9. Integrate Ethical Training: Participate in workshops, seminars, or online courses that focus on ethics in consulting. Formal training enhances your ethical acumen.

10. Develop Ethical Decision-Making Frameworks: Create a personal ethical decision-making framework that guides you through challenging situations. Consider the interests of all stakeholders involved.

By immersing yourself in a comprehensive exploration of ethical guidelines, you cultivate a heightened awareness of ethical considerations in your consulting practice. The journey of ethical understanding is one of continuous growth, reflection, and a commitment to uphold the highest standards of integrity, ensuring the utmost trust and respect from your clients and the consulting community at large.

Maintaining Confidentiality And Integrity

Maintaining confidentiality and integrity in your consulting business is not just a mere necessity; it is the bedrock upon which your reputation, client trust, and long-term success are built. Originality in upholding these principles showcases the significance through these insights:

1. Guardian of Trust: Confidentiality safeguards the sacred trust bestowed upon you by your clients. Your commitment to confidentiality becomes a guardian of their sensitive information, reinforcing the bond of trust.

2. Pillar of Credibility: Integrity cements your credibility as a consultant. Your unwavering commitment to ethical practices and moral conduct instills confidence in clients, setting you apart in a sea of consultants.

3. Cultivator of Relationships: Both confidentiality and integrity nurture enduring relationships. Clients seek partnerships with consultants who prioritize their interests and handle information with the utmost care.

4. Preserver of Confidential Insights: Confidentiality allows you to preserve your clients' unique insights and challenges, enabling you to deliver bespoke solutions tailored to their needs.

5. Enhancer of Decision-Making: Integrity empowers sound decision-making. Ethical conduct ensures your recommendations are rooted in genuine expertise, rather than influenced by personal gain.

6. Upholder of Industry Standards: Maintaining confidentiality and integrity contributes to raising the ethical bar across the consulting industry, reinforcing its credibility as a profession.

7. Advocate of Positive Reputation: Your steadfast commitment to these principles acts as an advocate for your consulting business, elevating its

reputation in the eyes of clients and peers alike.

8. Catalyst for Client Referrals: Clients who experience confidentiality and integrity firsthand become loyal advocates, generating word-of-mouth referrals that expand your client base.

9. Resilient Crisis Mitigator: Confidentiality protects your clients' interests during crises. When they face challenges, your integrity assures them of your steadfast support.

10. Fostering a Culture of Trust: Cultivating a culture of confidentiality and integrity within your consulting business encourages your team members to embody these principles, strengthening the consultancy as a whole.

In essence, maintaining confidentiality and integrity in your consulting business is not just a virtue; it is an inherent source of competitive advantage. As you embody these principles with originality, you fortify your consulting business as a trusted advisor, guided by ethical excellence and an unwavering commitment to preserving the sanctity of client relationships.

Navigating Potential Conflicts Of Interest

Navigating potential conflicts of interest with clients in your consulting business demands a delicate dance of transparency, ethical discernment, and client-focused decision-making. Embark on this journey with originality through these steps:

1. Proactive Disclosure: Disclose any potential conflicts of interest to clients from the outset. Transparently communicate relevant affiliations, relationships, or financial interests that could impact your objectivity.

2. Client-Centric Focus: Prioritize the interests and objectives of your clients above all else. Make decisions that align solely with their best interests, ensuring impartiality and ethical conduct.

3. Establish Boundaries: Set clear boundaries between personal interests and professional engagements. Avoid any activities that could compromise the integrity of your consulting services.

4. Evaluate Potential Risks: Thoroughly assess any situations that may pose conflicts of interest. Evaluate the potential risks and implications for your clients and your reputation.

5. Involve Third Parties: Consider engaging a neutral third party to evaluate potential conflicts of interest objectively. Their input can provide an unbiased perspective on the situation.

6. Implement Conflict Resolution Protocols: Develop robust conflict resolution protocols within your consulting business. These protocols guide your response to conflicts and prevent their escalation.

7. Step Back when Necessary: If a conflict of interest arises that could compromise your ability to act impartially, consider stepping back from the engagement to preserve integrity.

8. Seek Legal Advice: Consult legal professionals to understand the legal implications of potential conflicts of interest in your consulting practice.

9. Continuous Self-Assessment: Continuously assess your actions and decisions to ensure they align with your ethical standards. Regular self-reflection helps maintain ethical clarity.

10. Ethical Leadership: Promote a culture of ethical leadership within your consulting team. Foster open communication and encourage team members to address potential conflicts proactively.

Navigating conflicts of interest demands unwavering commitment to ethical conduct, putting your clients' interests front and center. By approaching these situations with transparency and integrity, you reinforce your consulting business as a trusted advisor, dedicated to delivering impartial and client-centric solutions. Originality lies in your proactive approach to conflict resolution, ensuring that ethical excellence becomes an indelible hallmark of your consultancy's legacy.

* * *

CHAPTER 11: CONTINUOUS LEARNING AND PROFESSIONAL DEVELOPMENT

The Importance Of Ongoing Learning And Staying Updated

In the realm of consulting, ongoing learning and staying updated are not just optional pursuits; they are the very lifeblood that keeps your expertise relevant, your solutions innovative, and your consulting business at the forefront of success. The importance of these endeavors can be emphasized through these original insights:

1. Relevance in a Dynamic Landscape: Ongoing learning ensures that your skills and knowledge remain current and relevant in an ever-evolving business landscape. It empowers you to adapt swiftly to emerging trends and client needs.

2. Innovative Solutions: Staying updated fosters a culture of innovation in your consulting business. Embracing new ideas and technologies enables you to craft cutting-edge solutions that captivate clients and outpace competitors.

3. Empowering Client Impact: Continuous learning empowers you to provide clients with well-informed and forward-thinking advice. By being well-versed in industry advancements, you become a transformative partner in their success journey.

4. Enhancing Professional Credibility: A commitment to ongoing learning elevates your professional credibility. Clients are more likely to trust consultants who demonstrate a thirst for knowledge and a dedication to staying informed.

5. Navigating Disruption with Confidence: As industries undergo disruption, ongoing learning equips you with the resilience to navigate turbulent times with confidence. Knowledge becomes the compass that guides your consulting strategies.

6. Attracting Top Clients: Clients seek consultants who offer valuable insights and innovative approaches. Staying updated helps you attract top clients who value your expertise and cutting-edge perspective.

7. Unlocking New Opportunities: As you expand your skill set, you unlock new opportunities for your consulting business. Diversifying your offerings opens doors to different markets and industries.

8. Adapting to Client Diversity: Every client is unique, and ongoing learning allows you to address their diverse challenges effectively. Versatility becomes a hallmark of your consulting prowess.

9. Fostering a Learning Culture: Embracing ongoing learning fosters a learning culture within your team. Encourage team members to pursue continuous development, igniting a spark of excellence throughout the consultancy.

10. Personal Fulfillment: Learning is an enriching and fulfilling journey. The pursuit of knowledge ignites passion and curiosity, inspiring consultants to push their own boundaries and achieve remarkable feats.

In the dynamic realm of consulting, where success hinges on expertise and adaptability, ongoing learning becomes a beacon that illuminates your path to sustained growth. Embrace the originality of this transformative journey, and your consulting business will shine as a beacon of knowledge and innovation in a world that thrives on progress and evolution.

Joining Professional Associations And Networks

Joining professional associations and networks can act as a potent elixir that nurtures the growth, credibility, and impact of your consulting business. Here's an original exploration of the benefits:

1. Amplified Visibility: Professional associations and networks provide a stage to showcase your consulting expertise to a broader audience. Increased visibility translates into a greater pool of potential clients and collaborations.

2. Nurturing Industry Relationships: Membership in these communities facilitates meaningful connections with like-minded professionals and industry leaders. Networking becomes an avenue to foster collaborative partnerships and exchange insights.

3. Continuous Learning: Engaging with peers in professional associations and networks opens doors to continuous learning. Workshops, seminars, and shared experiences enrich your knowledge, enhancing your consulting acumen.

4. Access to Resources: Professional associations often offer valuable resources, including research papers, industry reports, and best practices. These resources equip you with the latest tools and data to enhance your services.

5. Credential Reinforcement: Association membership enhances your consulting business's credibility. Clients value consultants who are part of respected organizations, providing a competitive edge in the market.

6. Referral Opportunities: Through networks, you gain access to a pool of professionals who may refer clients to your services. Positive relationships within these circles can lead to lucrative referrals.

7. Influencing Industry Direction: Active involvement in professional associations allows you to contribute to industry discussions and shape its future direction. Your voice becomes a driving force in consulting progress.

8. Client Assurance: Membership in reputable associations signals your commitment to ethical practices and professional standards. Clients find reassurance in working with consultants who align with respected industry values.

9. Peer Support and Encouragement: In challenging moments, these communities offer peer support and encouragement. Connecting with others who understand your consulting journey fosters resilience and motivation.

10. Global Reach: Some associations have a global presence, opening doors to international opportunities. Expanding your reach beyond borders broadens your potential client base.

By joining professional associations and networks, your consulting business thrives within a nurturing ecosystem of knowledge, connections, and shared vision. Originality lies in the unique bonds formed within these communities, elevating your consulting practice to new heights of success and impact, fueled by the collective spirit of collaboration and growth.

Pursuing Certifications And Further Education

Embrace the transformative power of certifications and further education as the catalysts that fuel your consulting business to ascend to new pinnacles of excellence and innovation. In this original journey of growth, consider these insights:

1. Elevating Expertise: Pursuing certifications and further education equips you with a treasure trove of specialized knowledge and advanced skills. Your expertise soars to new heights, distinguishing you as a sought-after consultant in your field.

2. Confidence Booster: Empower yourself with the confidence that comes from comprehensive learning. Each certification and educational milestone reinforces your abilities, inspiring a sense of self-assurance in your consulting prowess.

3. Adapting to Change: The landscape of consulting constantly evolves, and ongoing education helps you navigate these shifts with agility. Remaining current in best practices and industry trends enables you to thrive amidst change.

4. Relevance in Client Solutions: Certifications and further education enable you to offer cutting-edge solutions to your clients. Your enriched knowledge translates into innovative strategies that cater to their evolving needs.

5. Credential of Trust: Certifications are a badge of trust that clients seek in consultants. Demonstrating your commitment to continuous learning cultivates a reputation of reliability and expertise, attracting discerning clients.

6. Networking Opportunities: Pursuing certifications opens doors to valuable networking opportunities. Engaging with peers and experts fosters collaborative relationships that nurture both personal and business growth.

7. Diversified Offerings: Each new certification expands your service offerings. Diversifying your portfolio enriches your value proposition,

catering to a broader range of clients and industries.

8. Embracing a Growth Mindset: The pursuit of further education instills a growth mindset in your consulting business. Embracing the journey of learning fosters curiosity, resilience, and the pursuit of excellence.

9. Gaining an Edge in Competition: In a competitive consulting landscape, certifications provide a tangible advantage. They set you apart from competitors, positioning you as a consultant who continuously seeks improvement.

10. Fulfillment in Mastery: Beyond the professional benefits, certifications and further education offer personal fulfillment. The pursuit of knowledge becomes an ever-enriching journey that fuels your passion for consulting.

As you embark on this original path of professional growth, embrace certifications and further education as your guiding stars, illuminating a future of limitless possibilities for your consulting business. These transformative endeavors propel you towards a realm of elevated expertise, client satisfaction, and fulfillment, marking your consultancy as an influential beacon of knowledge and innovation.

* * *

CHAPTER 12: BUILDING A SUSTAINABLE AND FULFILLING CONSULTING BUSINESS

Achieving Work-Life Balance As A Consultant

Achieving work-life balance as a consultant requires the orchestration of an original symphony that harmonizes professional excellence with personal well-being. Navigate this virtuoso performance with these insightful steps:

1. Define Your Priorities: Identify your core values and priorities in both work and life. Embrace these anchors as guiding stars to steer your actions and decisions towards equilibrium.

2. Establish Boundaries: Set clear boundaries between work and personal time. Designate specific hours for work and cherish dedicated moments for family, hobbies, and self-care.

3. Embrace Flexibility: Embrace the flexibility of consulting by structuring your schedule to accommodate personal commitments. This fluidity empowers you to savor both professional and personal milestones.

4. Practice Mindful Presence: Embrace mindfulness in your daily life. Be fully present in each moment, whether it's engaging with clients or enjoying cherished moments with loved ones.

5. Delegate and Collaborate: Embrace the power of delegation and collaboration. Surround yourself with a reliable team or partner with fellow consultants to share the workload and ensure mutual support.

6. Efficiency Over Perfection: Prioritize efficiency over perfection. Set realistic expectations and avoid overcommitting, allowing you to deliver quality work without sacrificing personal time.

7. Unplug and Recharge: Unplug from work regularly to recharge your mind and body. Engage in activities that bring joy and relaxation, nurturing your creativity and mental well-being.

8. Exercise and Stay Active: Incorporate regular physical activity into your routine. Exercise not only improves your health but also boosts energy levels and enhances productivity.

9. Learn to Say No: Learn to gracefully decline opportunities or projects that may disrupt your work-life balance. Saying no allows you to protect your well-being and prioritize existing commitments.

10. Celebrate Achievements: Celebrate your professional achievements and personal milestones. Acknowledge your successes and indulge in self-appreciation, fostering a positive mindset.

In your original pursuit of work-life balance, you craft a symphony where your consulting expertise and personal well-being blend harmoniously. By tending to both facets with care and intention, you create a life of fulfillment and contentment, positioning yourself as a consultant who not only excels professionally but also cherishes the rhythm of life.

Creating A Positive Company Culture

Creating a positive company culture in your consulting business involves orchestrating a unique tapestry of values, collaboration, and shared purpose. Embark on this original journey with these transformative steps:

1. Craft a Compelling Vision: Set an inspiring vision that resonates with your team, aligning them on a collective purpose. This shared vision becomes the heartbeat of your positive company culture.

2. Foster Open Communication: Cultivate an environment where open communication flows freely. Encourage feedback, active listening, and the exchange of ideas, fostering a sense of inclusion and empowerment.

3. Nurture a Growth Mindset: Instill a growth mindset within your team, emphasizing that challenges are opportunities for learning and development. Embrace mistakes as stepping stones towards progress.

4. Lead by Example: Be the conductor of your company culture by exemplifying the values and principles you wish to instill. Demonstrate authenticity, integrity, and enthusiasm, inspiring your team to follow suit.

5. Recognize and Celebrate: Celebrate individual and team achievements, acknowledging their contributions to the company's success. Recognition fuels motivation and reinforces a culture of appreciation.

6. Promote Work-Life Integration: Embrace work-life integration over strict separation. Offer flexibility and support for personal commitments, nurturing a balanced and contented team.

7. Encourage Collaboration: Foster a culture of collaboration, where teamwork thrives and diverse perspectives contribute to creative solutions. Collaboration fuels innovation and a sense of camaraderie.

8. Invest in Professional Development: Invest in the growth of your team through continuous learning and professional development opportunities. Empower them to flourish as consultants and individuals.

9. Cultivate Empathy and Support: Foster empathy and support within your team. Create a safe space where team members feel comfortable seeking help and offering assistance to one another.

10. Infuse Fun and Inspiration: Infuse moments of joy, fun, and inspiration into your work environment. Encourage team-building activities and celebrate milestones with enthusiasm.

In this original symphony of a positive company culture, your consulting business thrives as a harmonious and empowered ensemble. By nurturing a culture where individuals are valued, growth is celebrated, and shared values guide every endeavor, you cultivate a consulting business that not only excels in its offerings but also fosters the well-being and fulfillment of your team.

Strategies For Long-Term Success And Personal Fulfillment

For long-term success and personal fulfillment in your consulting business, embark on a transformative expedition that blends originality, purposeful action, and self-awareness. Consider these strategic steps:

1. Unwavering Purpose: Define a purpose that ignites your passion and aligns with your values. Let it serve as the North Star that guides your decisions and fuels your commitment to long-term success.

2. Continual Adaptability: Embrace adaptability as a constant companion on your journey. Stay attuned to industry shifts, emerging trends, and client needs, adjusting your strategies accordingly.

3. Client-Centric Focus: Place clients at the heart of your consulting business. Nurture lasting relationships built on trust, empathy, and

delivering exceptional value.

4. Embrace Innovation: Embrace innovation as a driving force for progress. Foster a culture that encourages creative thinking, enabling you to craft groundbreaking solutions for your clients.

5. Strategic Partnerships: Forge strategic partnerships with complementary businesses or experts. Collaborate to amplify your reach, expand your offerings, and tap into new markets.

6. Invest in Talent: Attract and retain top talent that aligns with your company culture and values. Your team becomes a powerhouse of expertise and synergy, propelling long-term growth.

7. Rigorous Self-Assessment: Engage in regular self-assessment to identify areas for personal growth and development. Embrace a growth mindset that propels you towards continuous improvement.

8. Diversified Revenue Streams: Explore diversified revenue streams that expand your business's resilience. Offer a mix of services, products, and consulting formats that cater to different client needs.

9. Create a Learning Organization: Foster a learning organization that encourages knowledge-sharing, curiosity, and skill development. Invest in professional development for yourself and your team.

10. Balance and Well-being: Prioritize work-life balance and personal well-being. Embrace self-care practices that fuel your energy and foster resilience during challenging times.
11. Embrace Social Impact: Infuse a sense of purposeful social impact into your consulting business. Engage in initiatives that give back to the community and align with your values.

12. Celebrate Milestones: Celebrate your achievements and milestones along the way. Cultivate a culture that appreciates progress and recognizes efforts, fueling motivation for the long journey ahead.

In this original symphony of long-term success and personal fulfillment, you orchestrate a consulting business that not only thrives in the marketplace but also fulfills your vision for a purpose-driven and rewarding journey. By fusing these transformative strategies, you compose a legacy of lasting impact and prosperity in the dynamic realm of consulting.

Appendix:
Appendix: Resources for Aspiring Consultants

A. Recommended Reading List

Classic Books on Consulting
Business Strategy and Development
Communication and Presentation Skills
Marketing and Branding
Financial Management and Pricing Strategies

B. Useful Templates and Worksheets

Client Needs Assessment Worksheet
Consulting Proposal Template
Project Timeline and Milestones Worksheet
SWOT Analysis Template
Budgeting and Financial Planning Template

- Templates and resources for consulting proposals, contracts, and reports
- Case studies and real-life examples

And as an added bonus, scan the QR code below and get 10% off every t-shirt purchase. Simply apply the code BOOK at checkout.